FUN FACT FILE: US HISTORY!

20 FUN FACTS ABOUT THE SUPREME COURT

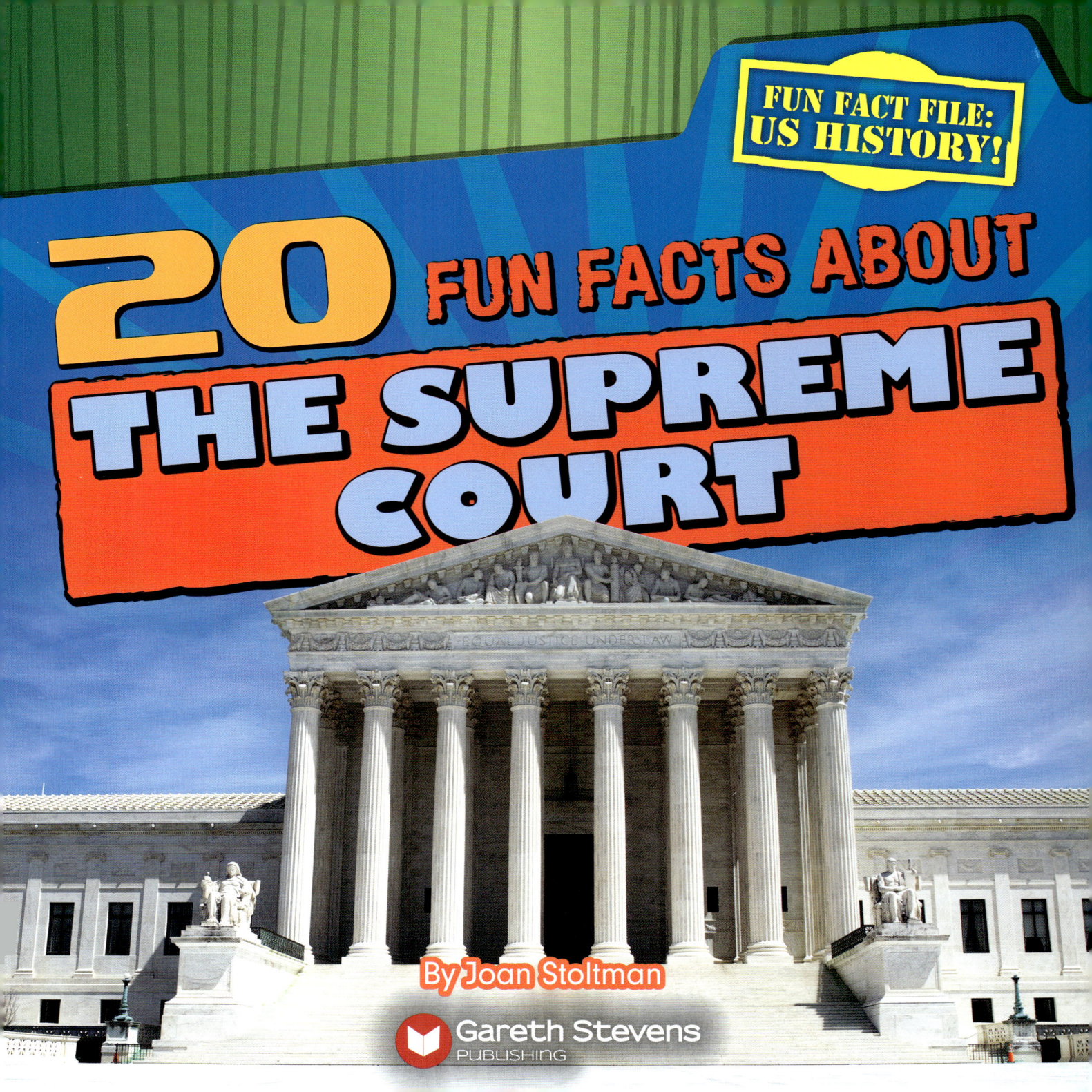

By Joan Stoltman

Gareth Stevens
PUBLISHING

Please visit our website, www.garethstevens.com. For a free color catalog of all our high-quality books, call toll free 1-800-542-2595 or fax 1-877-542-2596.

Library of Congress Cataloging-in-Publication Data

Names: Stoltman, Joan, author.
Title: 20 fun facts about the Supreme Court / Joan Stoltman.
Description: New York : Gareth Stevens Publishing, [2019] | Series: Fun fact file: US history! | Includes index.
Identifiers: LCCN 2018005940| ISBN 9781538219171 (library bound) | ISBN 9781538219157 (pbk.) | ISBN 9781538219164 (6 pack)
Subjects: LCSH: United States. Supreme Court–Juvenile literature. | United States. Supreme Court–Officials and employees–Juvenile literature.
Classification: LCC KF8742 .S76 2018 | DDC 347.73/26–dc23
LC record available at https://lccn.loc.gov/2018005940

Published in 2019 by
Gareth Stevens Publishing
111 East 14th Street, Suite 349
New York, NY 10003

Copyright © 2019 Gareth Stevens Publishing

Designer: Sarah Liddell
Editor: Mariel Bard

Photo credits: Cover, p. 1 Steven Frame/Shutterstock.com; p. 5 MCT/Contributor/Tribune News Service/Getty Images; p. 6 FastilyClone/Wikimedia Commons; p. 7 (both) Scewing/Wikimedia Commons; p. 8 Hank Walker/Contributor/The LIFE Picture Collection/Getty Images; p. 9 Corkythehornetfan/Wikimedia Commons; p. 10 (Antonin Scalia) Callinus/Wikimedia Commons; p. 10 (Clarence Thomas) Movieevery/Wikimedia Commons; p. 10 (David Souter) Manchiu/Wikimedia Commons; p. 11 MB298/Wikimedia Commons; p. 12 Naypong/Shutterstock.com; p. 13 Upstateherd/Wikimedia Commons; p. 14 Bettmann/Contributor/Bettmann/Getty Images; pp. 15, 22 Alex Wong/Staff/Getty Images News/Getty Images; p. 16 J.delanoy/Wikimedia Commons; p. 17 BrokenSphere/Wikimedia Commons; p. 18 Postdlf/Wikimedia Commons; p. 19 The Washington Post/Contributor/The Washington Post/Getty Images; p. 20 Howcheng/Wikimedia Commons; p. 21 Fœ/Wikimedia Commons; p. 23 David Hume Kennerly/Contributor/3rd Part - Misc/Getty Images; p. 24 Allmy/Shutterstock.com; p. 25 Andrew Redington/Staff/Getty Images Sport/Getty Images; p. 27 blambca/Shutterstock.com; p. 29 Travel Stock/Shutterstock.com.

Printed in the United States of America

CPSIA compliance information: Batch #CS18GS: For further information contact Gareth Stevens, New York, New York at 1-800-542-2595.

Contents

Words in the glossary appear in **bold** type the first time they are used in the text.

The Judicial Branch

The justices, or judges, of the United States Supreme Court have an important job. As the judicial, or law-making, branch of the US government, the Supreme Court **interprets** the Constitution and the laws made by Congress to make sure people's rights are kept safe. If they aren't, the Supreme Court can **overturn** a decision from any other court in the United States!

Each justice is appointed, or chosen, by the president, but the Senate votes on that choice. If the Senate approves, or accepts, the justice, they can have the job for life. Sometimes justices decide to step down, though.

The US government is made up of three branches, or parts: the legislative branch (Congress), the executive branch (the president), and the judicial branch (the Supreme Court).

Supreme Court **chamber**

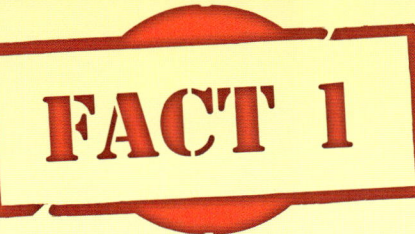

FACT 1

The Supreme Court didn't always have nine justices.

The Constitution didn't say how many justices should serve on the Supreme Court. It started in 1789 with six justices, but had between seven and 10 justices at different times over the next 80 years. In 1869, a law was passed to set it at nine.

In 1937, President Franklin D. Roosevelt wanted to be able to appoint more Supreme Court judges—up to 15! But Congress didn't allow it.

There is only one chief justice at a time, and this person is chosen by the president, just like the other justices. The other eight justices are known as associate justices.

John Jay

John Marshall

FACT 2

The court eras are named after the chief justice, who is in charge of the other justices.

The first court was called the Jay Court under Chief Justice John Jay. The Marshall Court lasted the longest at 34 years (1801–1835) under John Marshall.

So far, every justice was a lawyer before joining the Supreme Court!

It's not required that justices be lawyers or attend law school. In fact, there aren't any rules about who can be a justice. They can be any age, have any job, and be from anywhere—even outside the United States!

Before becoming a justice, Thurgood Marshall argued 32 cases in front of the Supreme Court. In 1967, he joined the other side of the bench as the first African American justice!

Each justice has four clerks, and they're all sworn to secrecy!

The 36 clerks work very closely with the justices on Supreme Court cases. To keep everything secret, clerks sometimes work on computers with no internet. They also eat separately from everyone else at work!

Some justices once worked as Supreme Court law clerks, including Chief Justice Roberts and Justices Breyer, Kagan, and Gorsuch.

In 2001, three justices recused, or removed, themselves from a case.

If a justice has any personal connection to a case, it wouldn't be fair for them to give an opinion. For the 2001 case, Antonin Scalia, David Souter, and Clarence Thomas all recused themselves, leaving only six justices on the bench.

Clarence Thomas

David Souter

Antonin Scalia

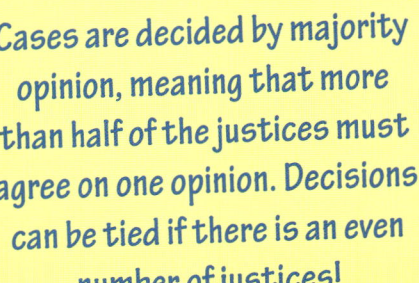

Cases are decided by majority opinion, meaning that more than half of the justices must agree on one opinion. Decisions can be tied if there is an even number of justices!

Neil M. Gorsuch (left) became a Supreme Court justice in 2017 after being nominated by President Trump.

As of 2017, seven people have declined service on the Supreme Court after being picked by a president!

Just because the president selects someone doesn't mean that person has to agree to serve. Even if a **nominee** does agree, the Senate might not approve! This has happened 12 times so far.

FACT 7

There's a basketball court on the top floor of the Supreme Court Building!

The Supreme Court didn't have its own building until 1935. Then, in the 1940s, a spare room was turned into a gym so workers, including justices, could exercise.

Because the basketball court is on the top floor—above the actual courtroom—it's often called the "highest court in the land"!

The inn had 141 rooms, four cottages, and a golf course! But the court never needed to use any of it.

FACT 8

The Supreme Court's emergency meeting place during the Cold War was a fancy hotel.

During the 1950s and 1960s, each of the three branches of government had bunkers, or secret shelters, to keep the government running in the event of an attack. The Supreme Court chose the Grove Park Inn in Asheville, North Carolina!

Bork lost the nomination with a vote of 58–42, which is the biggest defeat in Supreme Court history.

FACT 9

The word "bork" comes from Robert Bork, whom the Senate refused to approve as a Supreme Court justice!

Bork's strong opinions made many people, including some senators, angry. So his **opponents** ganged up on him. Their goal was to ruin his chances of winning by arguing against him—and that's exactly what "borking" means!

FACT 10

One justice didn't ask a single question during oral arguments for 10 years!

From February 22, 2006, until February 29, 2016, Justice Clarence Thomas sat silent during oral arguments. For all those years, the only time he spoke up was to tell a joke!

Justice Thomas believed the other justices asked plenty of questions already, so he didn't feel he needed to ask more.

FACT 11

The first nominee to be refused by the Senate had already served on the first Supreme Court!

George Washington had chosen John Rutledge as an associate justice in 1790, but by 1791, Rutledge left the court. Then, in 1795, he wanted to be chief justice, but Congress voted no.

Rutledge served as a backup chief justice while the court was on a break—which is the closest he ever got to having the job.

William Howard Taft was the first—and only—person to serve as both president and Supreme Court justice.

During his presidency from 1909 to 1913, Taft chose five justices and a chief justice for the court. Then, in 1921, Taft was appointed to the Supreme Court by President Warren Harding. Taft served as chief justice for 9 years.

Taft liked being chief justice much more than he liked being president!

Only four women have served as Supreme Court justices (left to right): Sandra Day O'Connor, Sonia Sotomayor, Ruth Bader Ginsburg, and Elena Kagan.

FACT 13

The first woman justice was confirmed by a unanimous Senate vote!

In 1981, Sandra Day O'Connor was approved by a vote of 99–0, with one senator not present to vote. She served for 24 years, retiring in January 2006.

FACT 14

All the justices wear black robes in court, but no one really knows why!

Since around 1800, black has been the color of choice. Nothing says they have to wear black, and some justices have added **embellishments** to their robes, like stripes or special collars.

Ruth Bader Ginsburg is known for her many fancy collars. She wears certain ones on certain days, but this white beaded collar is her favorite.

19

All nine justices shake hands before going into the courtroom and before discussions in their meeting room.

Chief Justice Melville W. Fuller, who served from 1888 to 1910, started this **tradition**. It's supposed to remind justices that, even if they have different views, they still share the same important job.

As different as their opinions might be, justices have a lot of respect for each other and sometimes become close friends.

The newest justice has to get coffee for the other justices when they're in their meeting room.

Called the junior associate justice, this person also takes notes, answers the door, and sends clerks to the library. Another duty is attending cafeteria committee meetings to talk about the food!

When Elena Kagan was the junior associate justice, she had a frozen yogurt machine installed in the Supreme Court dining area!

The runners are usually young reporters, and they often wear sneakers when they know they'll be on the move!

FACT 17

When major Supreme Court decisions are announced, people sprint to deliver the news!

Cameras aren't allowed in the courtroom, so decisions are printed out instead. To get the information to news reporters, workers run as fast as they can from the Supreme Court Building to the street, where TV cameras and reporters are waiting.

FACT 18

The Supreme Court is asked to hear around 8,000 cases each term, but justices select only about 80!

The term starts on the first Monday in October, and summer break starts in July. To fit 80 cases into this schedule, lawyers only have 30 minutes each to argue their side.

Before and after oral arguments, the justices learn all they can about their cases in order to make the best decisions.

The Supreme Court decided that tomatoes are vegetables, but really they're fruits!

In 1893, John Nix argued that tomatoes are fruits and should not be taxed as vegetables, according to a recent law. The Supreme Court disagreed, and ever since, there's been confusion over what a tomato really is!

In Justice Horace Gray's opinion, tomatoes should be considered vegetables because they're eaten at dinner, in soups, and with meat—not for dessert, like most fruits.

FACT 20

In 2001, the Supreme Court ruled in favor of golf carts!

Golfer Casey Martin wanted to play in the PGA Tour, a big golf event. But Martin has a disability that makes walking hard, so he needs a golf cart. The PGA thought this was unfair to other golfers, but the Supreme Court ruled in Martin's favor.

US Circuit Courts

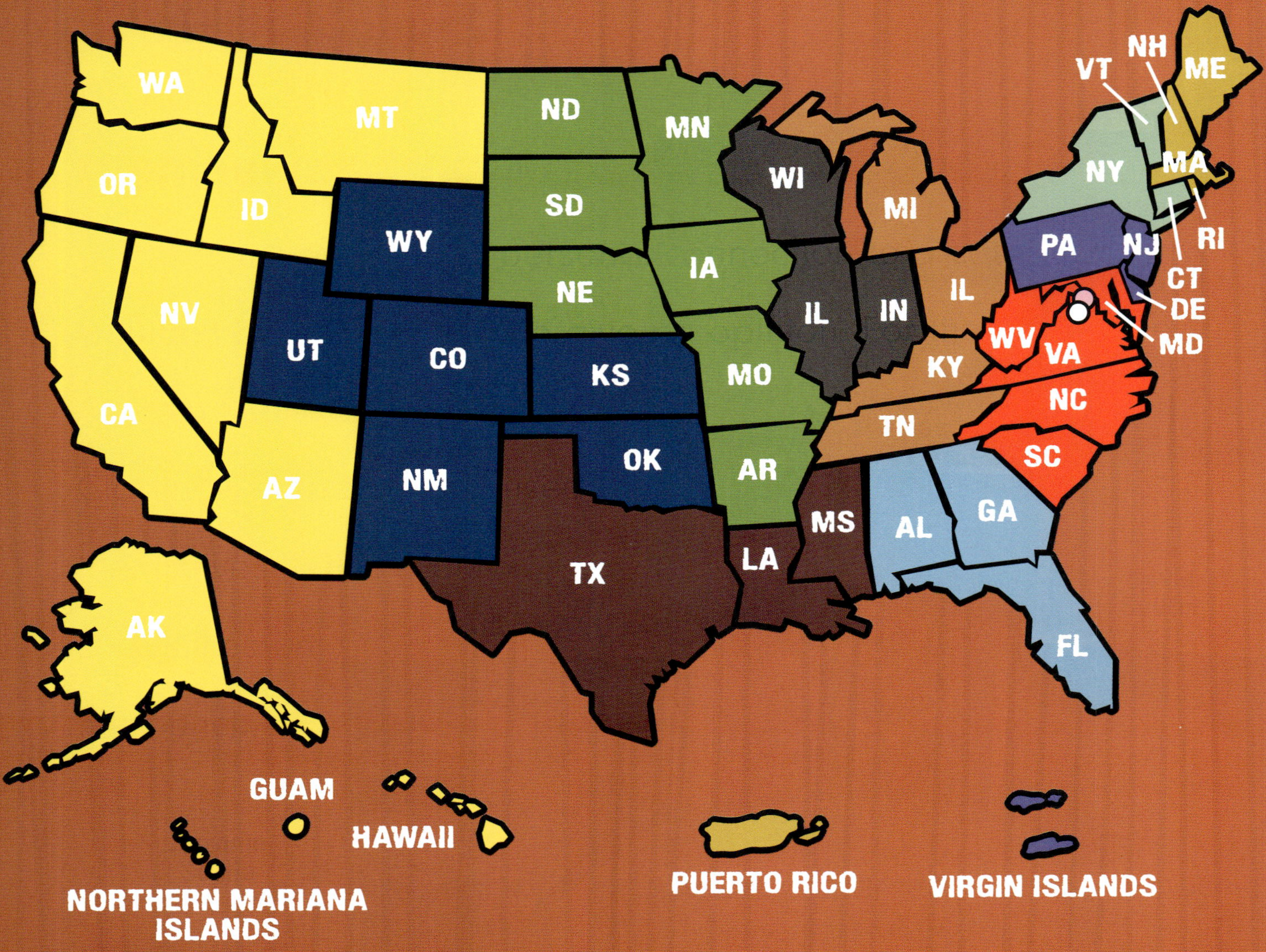

Along with their duties in the Supreme Court, each justice is also assigned to at least one of the 13 circuit courts. These courts hear appeals, or cases that one side wants retried in hopes of receiving a different outcome.

CHIEF JUSTICE JOHN ROBERTS: ■ FEDERAL CIRCUIT ■ DISTRICT OF COLUMBIA CIRCUIT ■ FOURTH CIRCUIT

ASSOCIATE JUSTICE STEPHEN BREYER: ■ FIRST CIRCUIT

ASSOCIATE JUSTICE RUTH BADER GINSBURG: ■ SECOND CIRCUIT

ASSOCIATE JUSTICE SAMUEL ALITO: ■ THIRD CIRCUIT ■ FIFTH CIRCUIT

ASSOCIATE JUSTICE ELENA KAGAN: ■ SIXTH CIRCUIT ■ SEVENTH CIRCUIT

ASSOCIATE JUSTICE NEIL GORSUCH: ■ EIGHTH CIRCUIT

ASSOCIATE JUSTICE ANTHONY KENNEDY: ■ NINTH CIRCUIT

ASSOCIATE JUSTICE SONIA SOTOMAYOR: ■ TENTH CIRCUIT

ASSOCIATE JUSTICE CLARENCE THOMAS: ■ ELEVENTH CIRCUIT

Visit the Supreme Court

Since it was created in 1789, the Supreme Court has heard many cases and made many important decisions that have shaped our country. Now that you've learned some exciting facts about the Supreme Court, you should see it for yourself!

Visiting the Supreme Court Building in Washington, DC, takes some planning. There's usually a line for the 250 public seats in the courtroom. There isn't much you can bring inside with you—including phones, books, and even sunglasses. But it's all worth it because watching the Supreme Court is seeing history in the making!

During your visit, you can also watch a movie about the Supreme Court and tour the courtroom—when it's empty, of course.

Glossary

accessible: able to be used

chamber: a large room where members of a government group have meetings

decline: to say that you will not or cannot do something

embellishment: a decoration or detail added to something

emergency: an unexpected situation that needs quick action

era: a period of time connected with a certain person or event

interpret: to tell the meaning of

lawyer: someone whose job it is to help people with their questions and problems with the law

nominee: someone who is suggested for a job or honor

opponent: a person or team you are against for a specific reason

oral: spoken

overturn: to decide that a ruling or decision is wrong and change it

tradition: a way of thinking, acting, or doing something that has been used by the people in a certain group for a long time

unanimous: with all members in agreement

For More Information

Books

Loria, Laura. *What Is the Judicial Branch?* New York, NY: Britannica Educational Publishing, 2016.

McAneney, Caitie. *Standing in a Supreme Court Justice's Shoes.* New York, NY: Cavendish Square Publishing, 2016.

Rose, Simon. *Supreme Court.* New York, NY: Smartbook Media Inc., 2016.

Websites

Members of the Supreme Court of the United States
www.supremecourt.gov/about/members.aspx
Slide the timeline back and forth to see where each justice fits in the history of the court.

Timeline of the Justices
supremecourthistory.org/history_timeline.html
Read short biographies of US Supreme Court justices. Many include recordings of the justices speaking.

Index